T0042532

**GUITAR TRANSCRIPTIONS
OF CLASSICS ARRANGED FOR
ROCK AND METAL GUITARISTS
INCLUDES TABLATURE**

2	**Introduction**	
3	**Classical Electric Playing Tips**	
5	**Symphony No. 25**	
6	**Quartet No. 14 In G Major**	
7	**Quartet No. 15 in D Minor**	
8	**Magic Flute Overture**	
9	**Minuet**	
11	**Orchestral Suite No. 3 in D Major**	
12	**Orchestral Suite No. 2 in B Minor**	
12	**Prelude Cello Suite VI**	
13	**Prelude Cello Suite III**	
14	**Bourée Lute Suite No. 1**	
15	**Brandenburg Concerto No. 5 in D Major**	
17	**Cello Suite VI Gavotte 2**	
18	**Caprice No. 24 Opus 1**	
19	**Caprice No. 2 Opus 1 (1st Excerpt)**	
20	**Caprice No. 21 Opus 1**	
20	**Caprice No. 2 Opus 1 (2nd Excerpt)**	
21	**Caprice No. 16 Opus 1 (1st Excerpt)**	Paganini
21	**Caprice No. 5 Opus 1**	Paganini
22	**Caprice No. 16 Opus 1 (2nd Exerpt)**	Paganini
22	**Caprice No. 1 Opus 1**	Paganini
23	**2nd Arabesque**	Debussy
24	**Claire de Lune**	Debussy
25	**Images**	Debussy
26	**Concerto In A Minor Opus 3 No. 8**	Vivaldi
29	**Bagatelles**	Beethoven
33	**Canon In D (Guitars I and II)**	Pachelbel
37	**Canon In D (Background Guitar)**	Pachelbel
39	**Le Coucou**	Daquin
48	**Caprice No. 5**	Paganini
55	**Caprice No. 16**	Paganini
59	**Bourée**	Bach
61	**Symphony No. 25**	Mozart

Editor's Note:
*Some artistic liberties have been
taken on the recording. Your
improvisation is also encouraged.*

To access audio, visit:
www.halleonard.com/mylibrary

Enter Code
6662-7761-2402-5364

ISBN: 978-0-7935-0273-8

Visit Hal Leonard Online at
www.halleonard.com

Contact Us:
Hal Leonard
7777 West Bluemound Road
Milwaukee, WI 53213
Email: info@halleonard.com

In Europe contact:
Hal Leonard Europe Limited
42 Wigmore Street
Marylebone, London, W1U 2RN
Email: info@halleonardeurope.com

In Australia contact:
Hal Leonard Australia Pty. Ltd.
4 Lentara Court
Cheltenham, Victoria, 3192 Australia
Email: info@halleonard.com.au

A different kind of guitar hero appeared in the '80s. Steep in the classical tradition, this new breed forged a soaring virtuoso style that left the old cliches in the dust.

I immediately made the connection between modern heroes like Yngwie Malmsteen and Randy Rhoads to the heroes of the past like Mozart, Bach, and Paganini.

With the creation of Challenge the Masters, it is my hope that you will discover new musical sounds and feelings as you electrify these classical riffs.

As Shakespeare once wrote: "Sound music and rock the ground."

Touché

Classical Electric Playing Tips

Muting, blocking, or stopping the sound of a string will help you get rid of unwanted buzz, overtones, clicks, scrapes, growls etc.

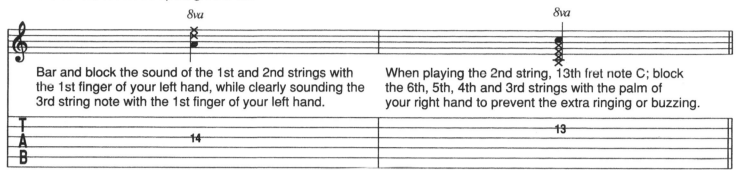

Bar and block the sound of the 1st and 2nd strings with the 1st finger of your left hand, while clearly sounding the 3rd string note with the 1st finger of your left hand.

When playing the 2nd string, 13th fret note C; block the 6th, 5th, 4th and 3rd strings with the palm of your right hand to prevent the extra ringing or buzzing.

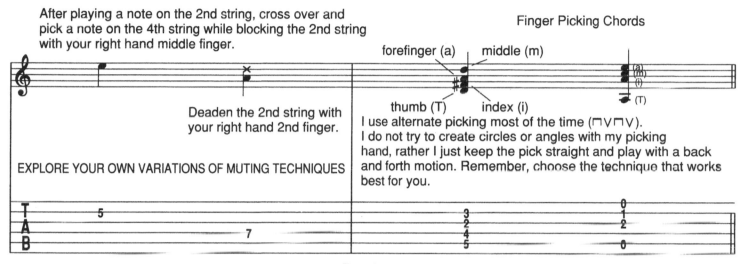

After playing a note on the 2nd string, cross over and pick a note on the 4th string while blocking the 2nd string with your right hand middle finger.

Deaden the 2nd string with your right hand 2nd finger.

EXPLORE YOUR OWN VARIATIONS OF MUTING TECHNIQUES

Finger Picking Chords

forefinger (a)   middle (m)

thumb (T)   index (i)

I use alternate picking most of the time (⊓∨⊓∨).
I do not try to create circles or angles with my picking hand, rather I just keep the pick straight and play with a back and forth motion. Remember, choose the technique that works best for you.

For pick sweeping I usually let the notes of a chord ring over one another in harmony rather than separating the sound of each note.

Scale Studies

Eb major
Scale study for Mozart section No. 1

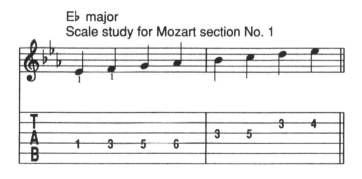

D Major
Scale study for Bach section No. 6

A Major
Scale study for Paganini section 5

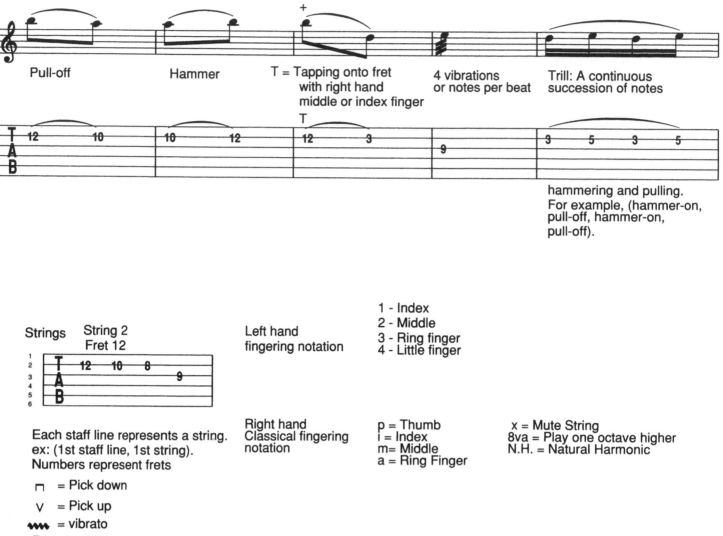

Pull-off

Hammer

T = Tapping onto fret
with right hand
middle or index finger

4 vibrations
or notes per beat

Trill: A continuous
succession of notes

hammering and pulling.
For example, (hammer-on,
pull-off, hammer-on,
pull-off).

Strings   String 2
           Fret 12

Each staff line represents a string.
ex: (1st staff line, 1st string).
Numbers represent frets

⊓ = Pick down

V = Pick up

〜〜 = vibrato

Left hand
fingering notation

Right hand
Classical fingering
notation

1 - Index
2 - Middle
3 - Ring finger
4 - Little finger

p = Thumb
i = Index
m= Middle
a = Ring Finger

x = Mute String
8va = Play one octave higher
N.H. = Natural Harmonic

For more basic notational information and explanations refer to the
Guitar Empire Rock Book.

Symphony No. 25

Wolfgang Amadeus Mozart
K. 183

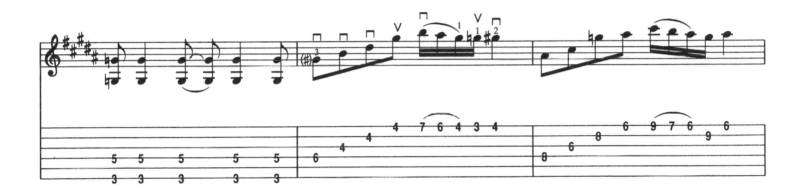

Quartet No. 14 In G Major

Wolfgang Amadeus Mozart
K. 387

1. "Haydn" Quartets

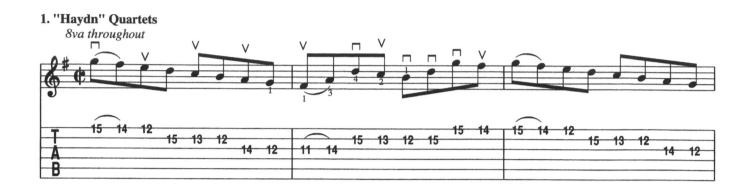

2. *8va throughout*

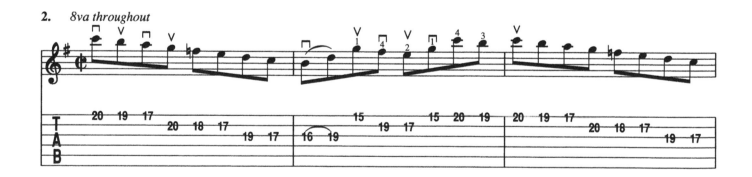

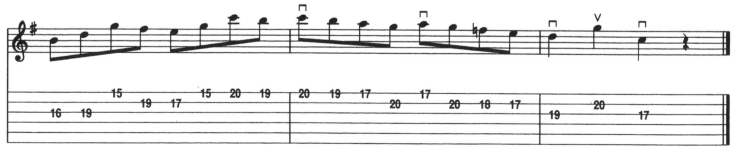

Quartet No. 15 In D Minor

Wolfgang Amadeus Mozart
K. 421

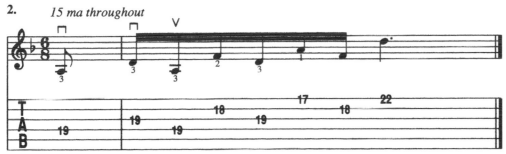

Magic Flute Overture

Wolfgang Amadeus Mozart

1.

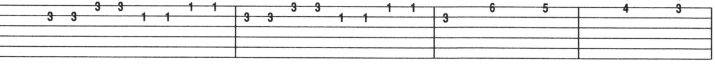

2. *(picking tremolo)*

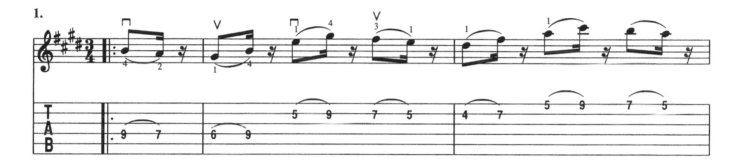

TRACK 6

Minuet

Wolfgang Amadeus Mozart

1.

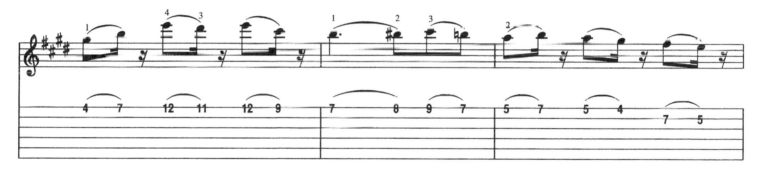

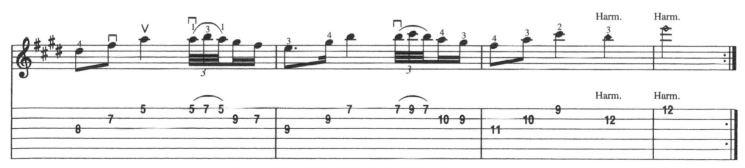

2.

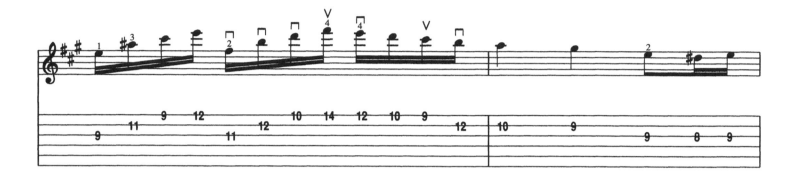

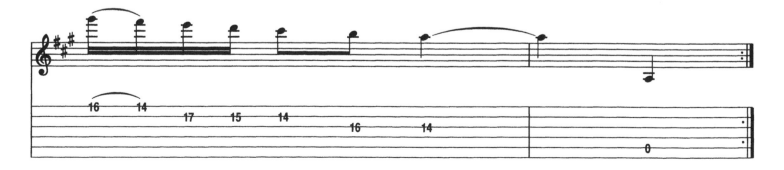

Orchestral Suite No. 3 In D Major

Johann Sebastian Bach

Orchestral Suite No. 2 In B Minor

Johann Sebastian Bach

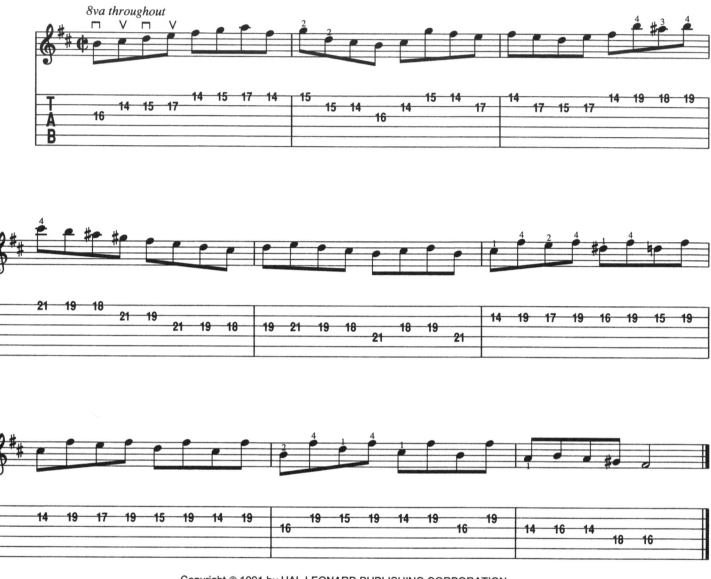

Prelude Cello Suite VI

Johann Sebastian Bach

TRACK 10

Prelude Cello Suite III

Johann Sebastian Bach

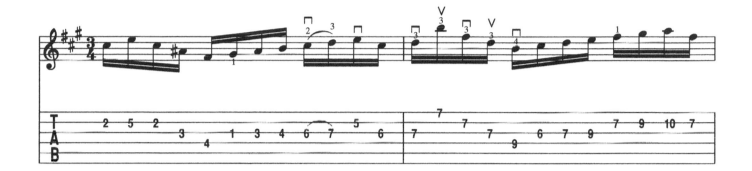

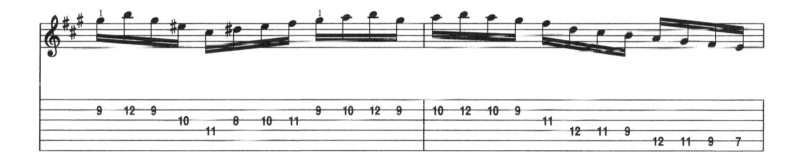

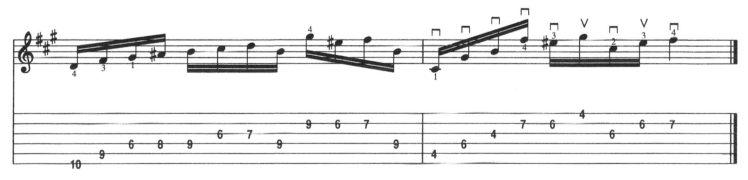

TRACK 11

Bourrée Lute Suite No. 1

Johann Sebastian Bach

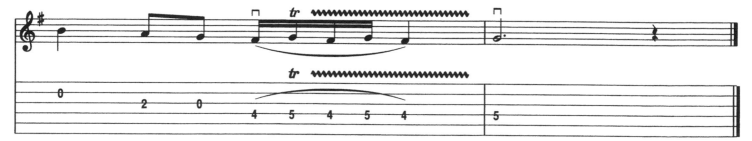

TRACK 12

Brandenburg Concerto
No. 5 In D Major

Johann Sebastian Bach

1.

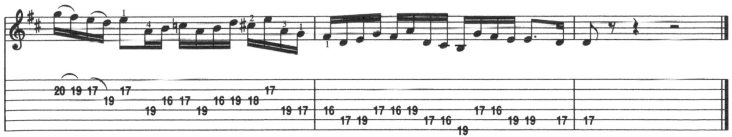

2.

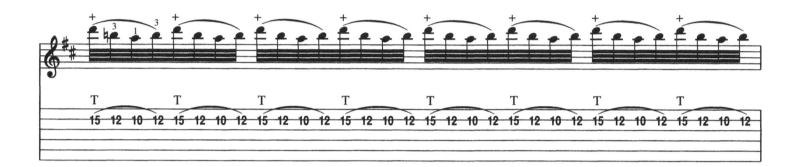

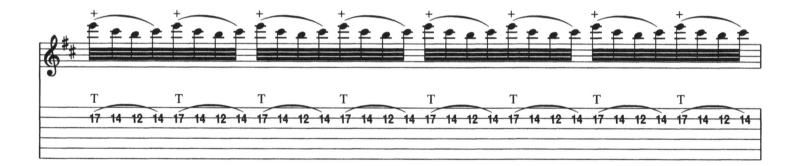

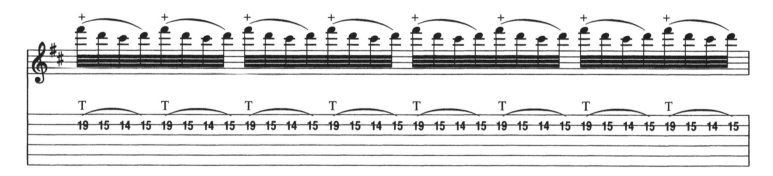

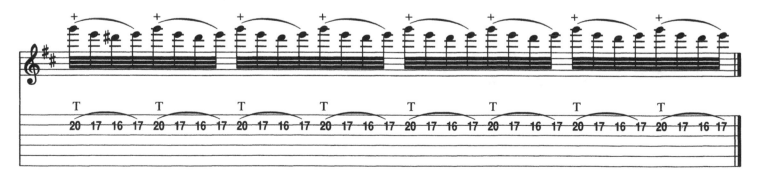

3.

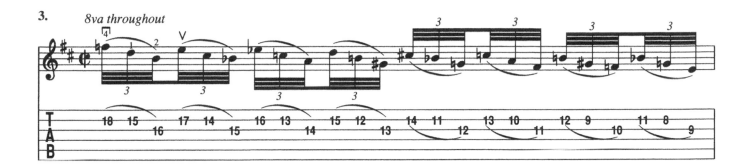

4.

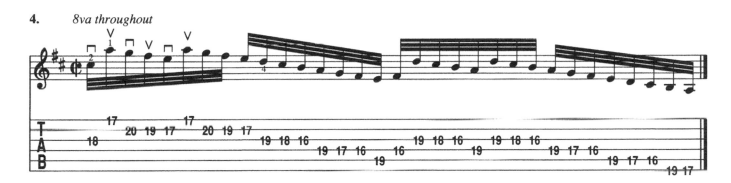

TRACK 13

Cello Suite VI
Gavotte 2

Johann Sebastian Bach

Caprice No. 24 Opus 1

Nicolò Paganini

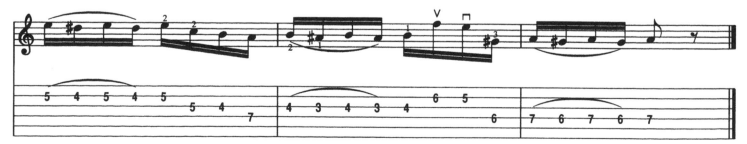

2.

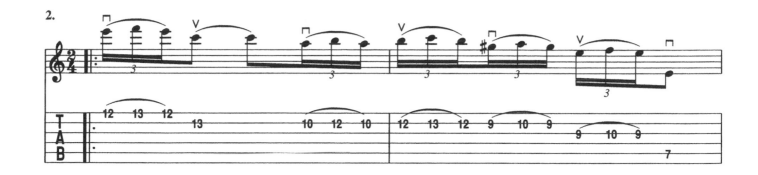

Caprice No. 2 Opus 1 (1st Excerpt)

Nicolò Paganini

TRACK 15

Caprice No. 21 Opus 1

Nicolò Paganini

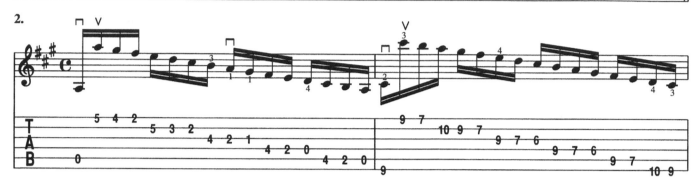

Caprice No. 2 Opus 1 (2nd Excerpt)

Nicolò Paganini

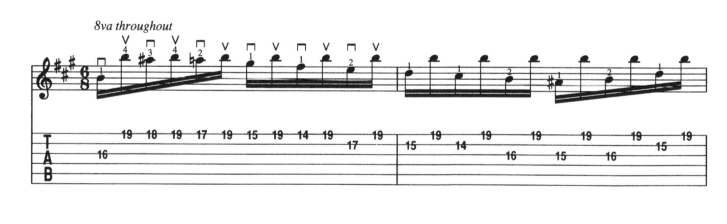

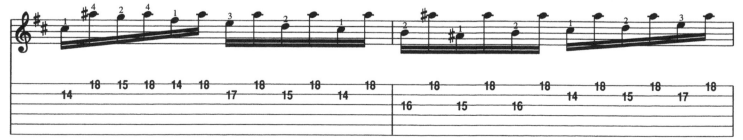

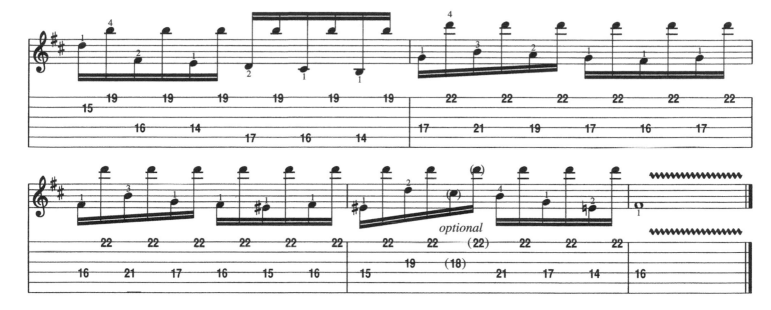

TRACK 18

Caprice No. 16 Opus 1 (1st Excerpt)

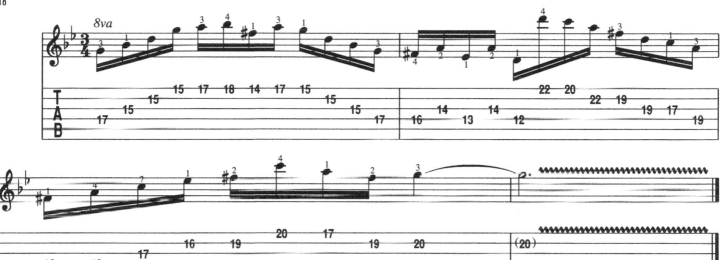

TRACK 19

Caprice No. 5 Opus 1

Nicolò Paganini

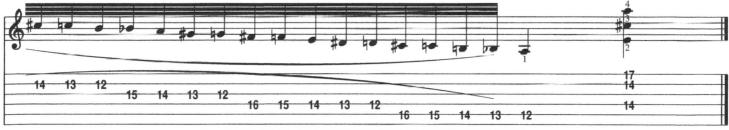

Caprice No. 16 Opus 1 (2nd Excerpt)

Nicolò Paganini

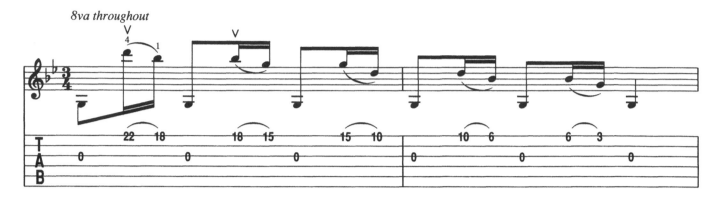

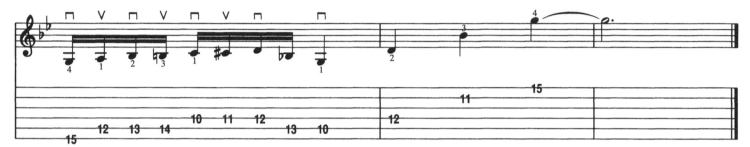

Caprice No. 1 Opus 1

Nicolò Paganini

2nd Arabesque

Claude Debussy

Claire de Lune

Claude Debussy

1.

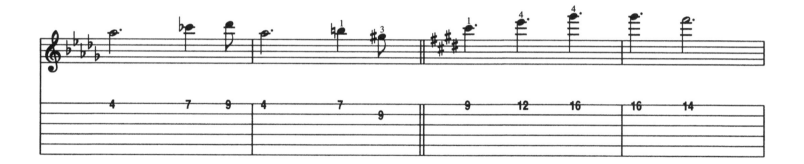

2.

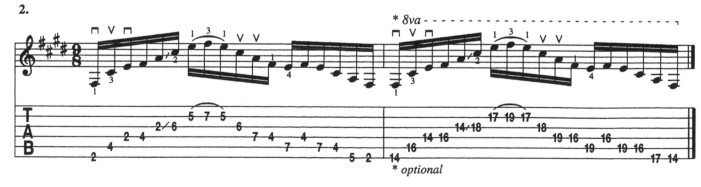

* optional

Images

Claude Debussy

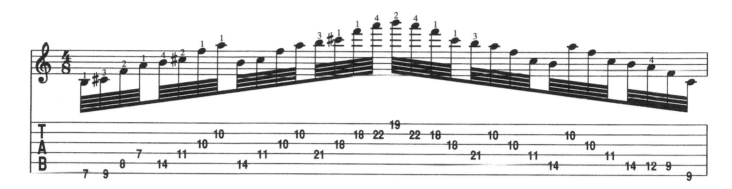

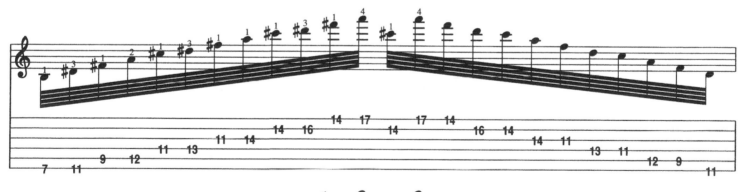

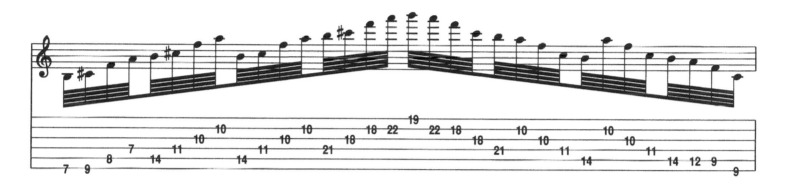

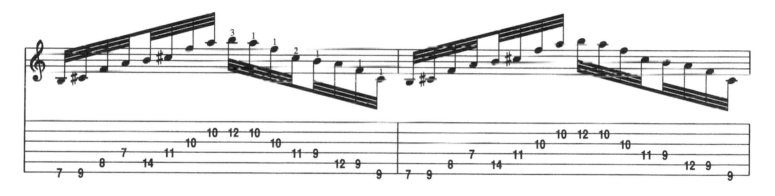

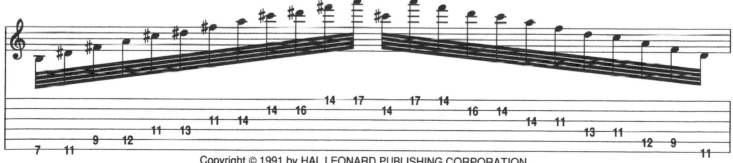

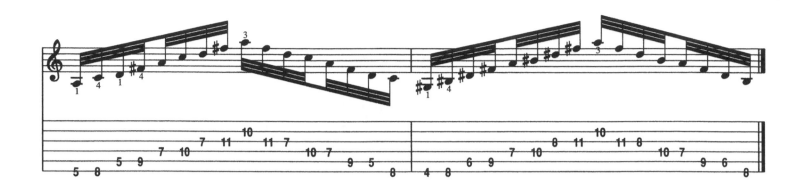

TRACK 25

Concerto In A Minor Opus 3 No. 8

Antonio Vivaldi

1. *8va throughout*

2. *8va throughout*

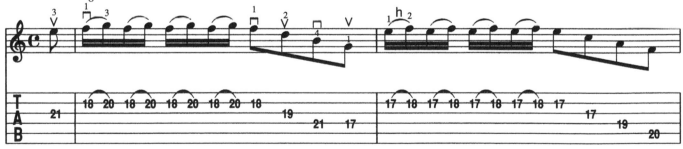

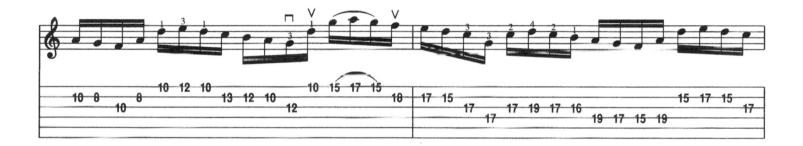

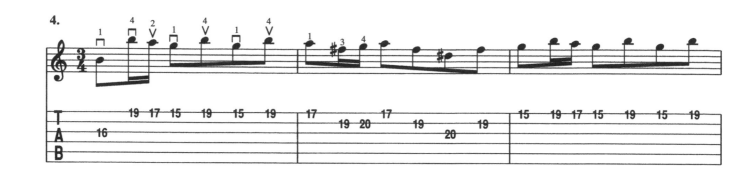

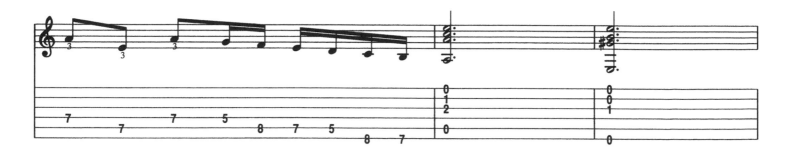

TRACK 26

Bagatelles

Ludwig van Beethoven

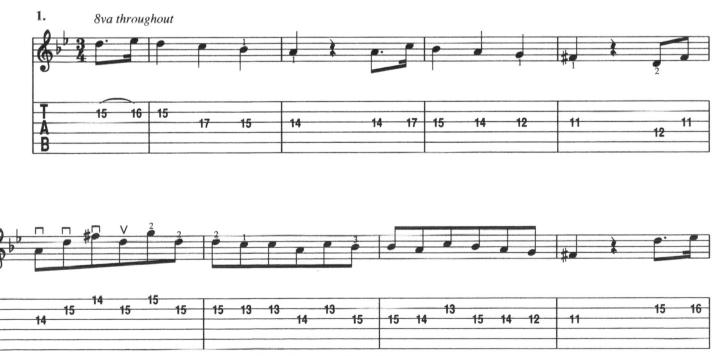

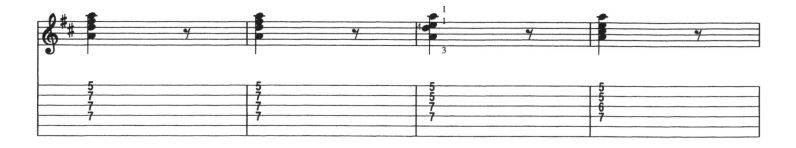

3.

4.

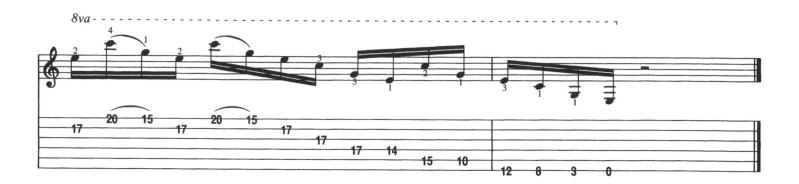

5.

Canon In D

Johann Pachelbel

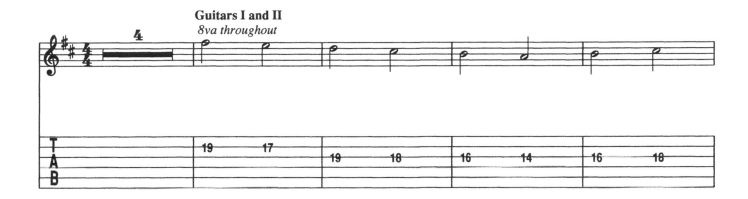

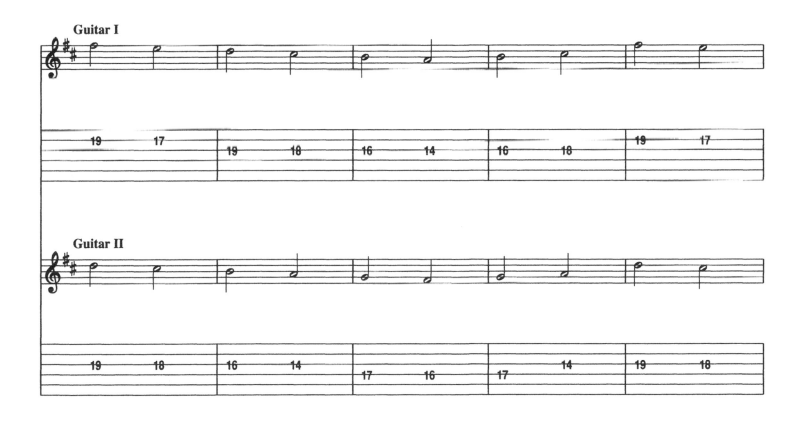

Guitars I and II

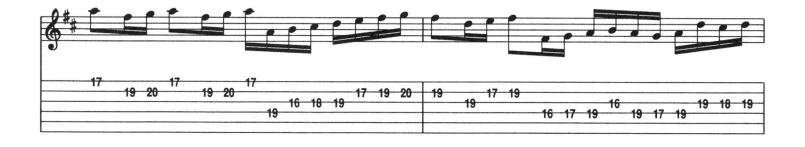

Guitar I

Guitar II

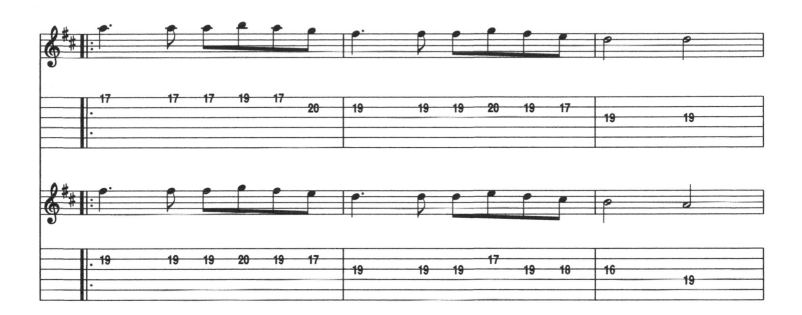

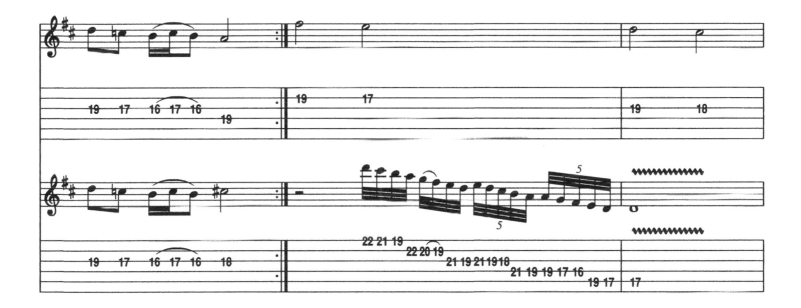

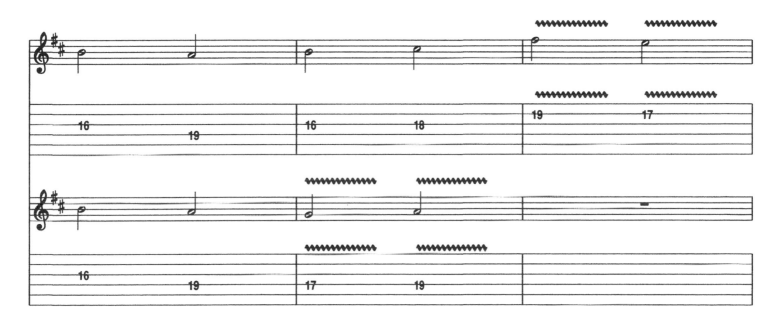

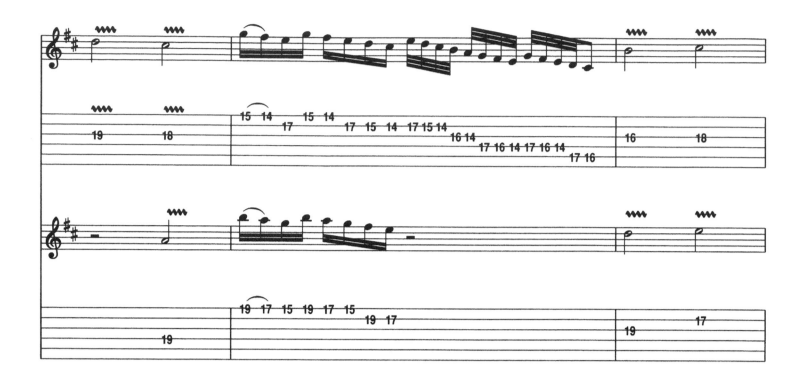

Guitars I and II

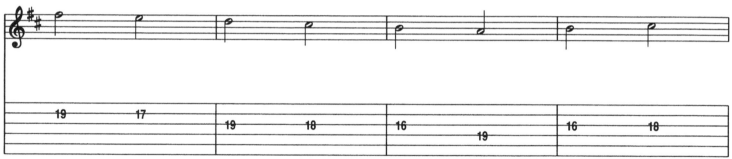

Guitar I

Guitar II

Canon In D

Johann Pachelbel

Background Guitar

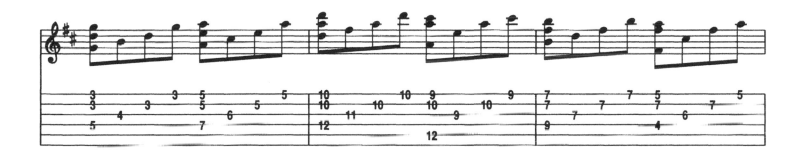

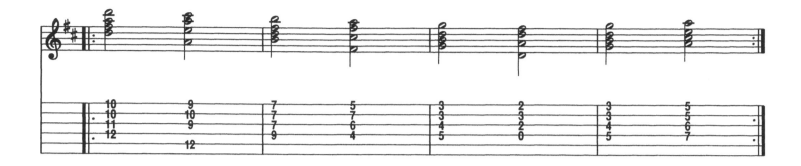

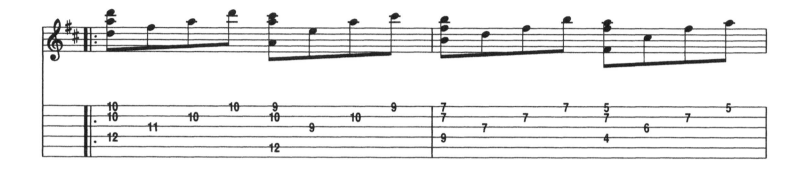

Le Coucou

Louis-Claude Daquin

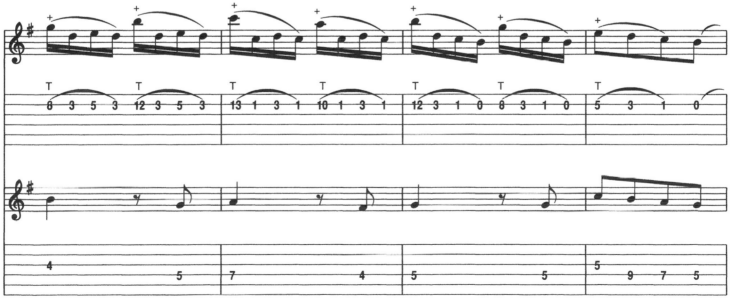

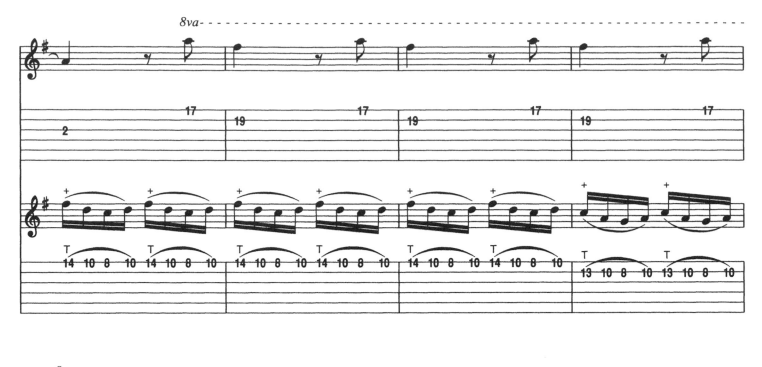

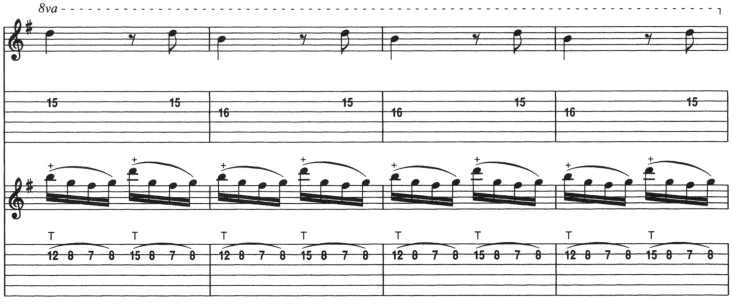

TRACK 29

Caprice No. 5

Nicolò Paganini

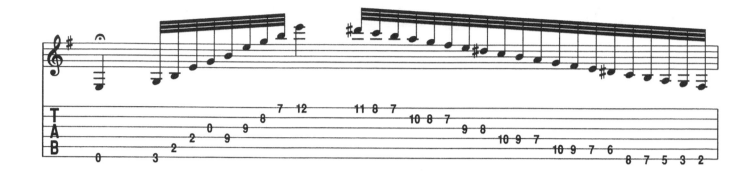

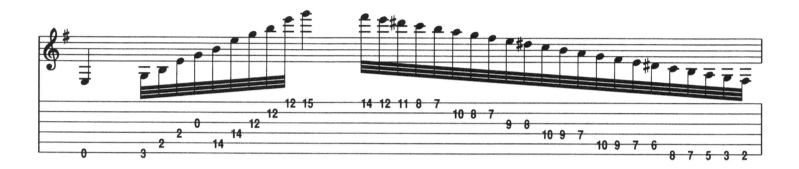

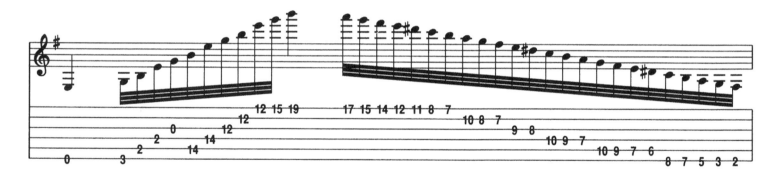

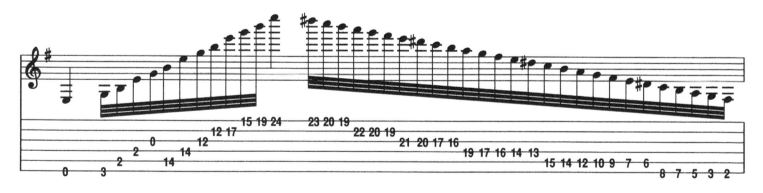

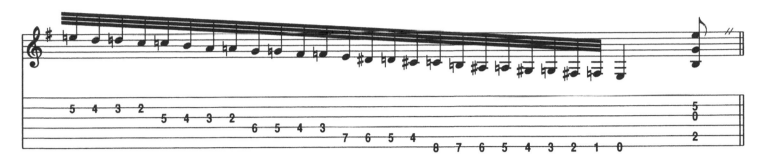

Agitato

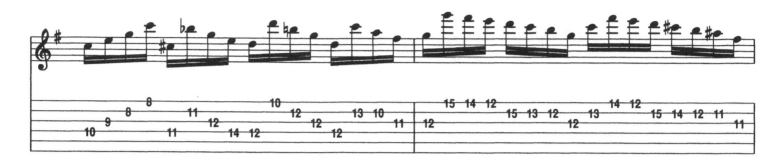

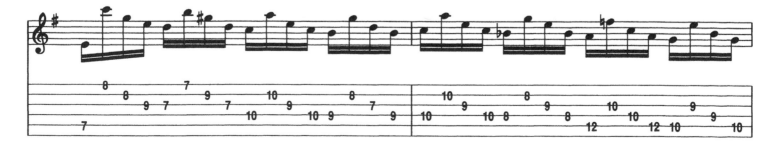

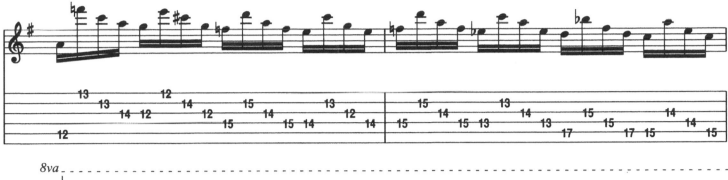

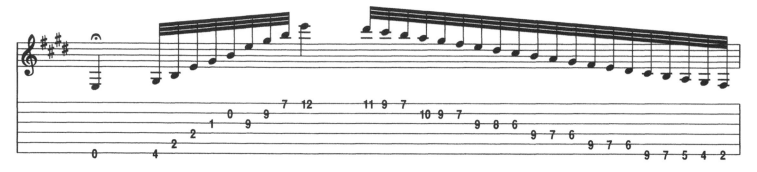

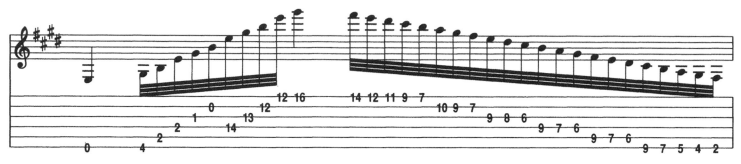

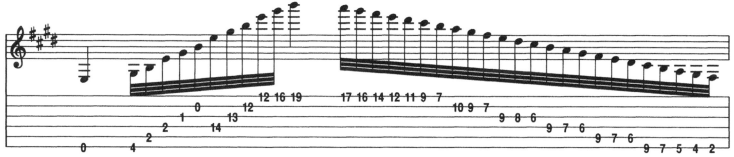

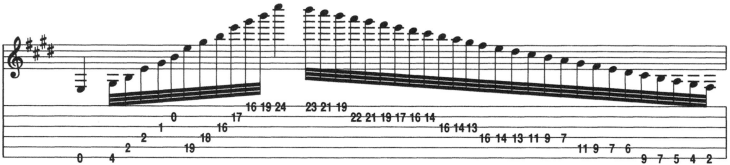

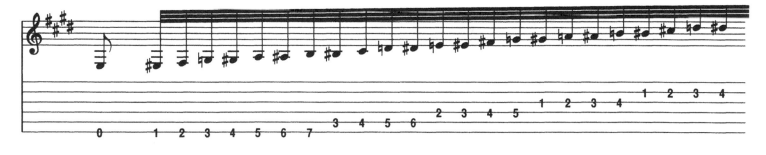

TRACK 30

Caprice No. 16

Nicolò Paganini

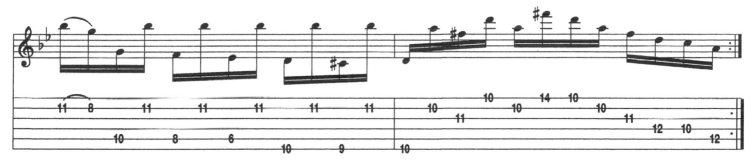

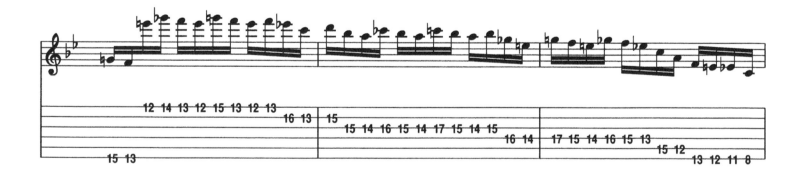

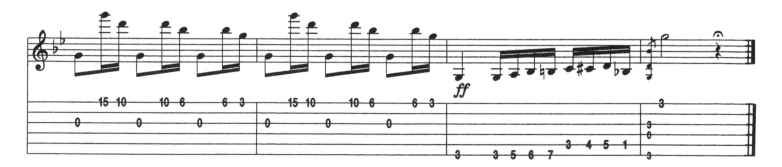

Bourrée

Johann Sebastian Bach

D.C. al Fine

Symphony No. 25

Wolfgang Amadeus Mozart

Gtr. 2 play one octave higher
Gtr. 1.

To Coda ⊕

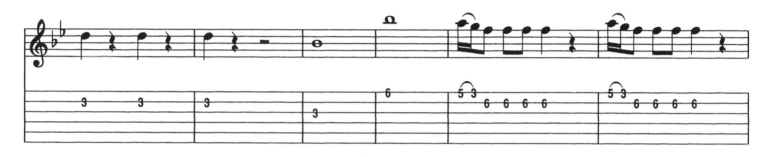

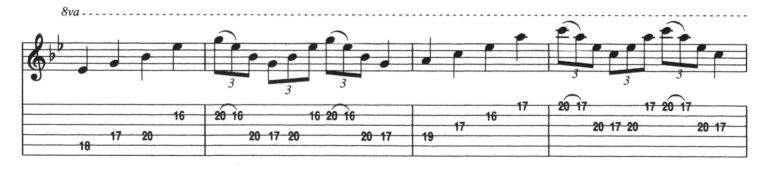

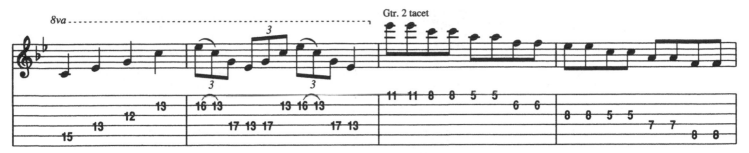

D.C. al Coda

Coda

CLASSICAL GUITAR

INSTRUCTIONAL BOOKS & METHODS AVAILABLE FROM HAL LEONARD

CLASSICAL STUDIES FOR PICK-STYLE GUITAR
by William Leavitt
Berklee Press
This Berklee Workshop, featuring over 20 solos and duets by Bach, Carcassi, Paganini, Sor and other renowned composers, is designed to acquaint intermediate to advanced pick-style guitarists with some of the excellent classical music that is adaptable to pick-style guitar. With study and practice, this workshop will increase a player's knowledge and proficiency on this formidable instrument.
50449440...$14.99

ÉTUDES SIMPLES FOR GUITAR
by Leo Brouwer
Editions Max Eschig
This new, completely revised and updated edition includes critical commentary and performance notes. Each study is accompanied by an introduction that illustrates its principal musical features and technical objectives, complete with suggestions and preparatory exercises.
50565810 Book/CD Pack.....................................$26.99

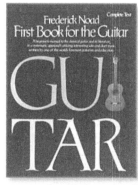

FIRST BOOK FOR THE GUITAR
by Frederick Noad
G. Schirmer, Inc.
A beginner's manual to the classical guitar. Uses a systematic approach using the interesting solo and duet music written by Noad, one of the world's foremost guitar educators. No musical knowledge is necessary. Student can progress by simple stages. Many of the exercises are designed for a teacher to play with the students. Will increase student's enthusiasm, therefore increasing the desire to take lessons.
50334370 Part 1.......................................$14.99
50334520 Part 2.......................................$18.99
50335160 Part 3.......................................$16.99
50336760 Complete Edition.............................$32.99

HAL LEONARD CLASSICAL GUITAR METHOD
by Paul Henry
This comprehensive and easy-to-use beginner's guide uses the music of the master composers to teach you the basics of the classical style and technique. Includes pieces by Beethoven, Bach, Mozart, Schumann, Giuliani, Carcassi, Bathioli, Aguado, Tarrega, Purcell, and more. Includes all the basics plus info on PIMA technique, two- and three-part music, time signatures, key signatures, articulation, free stroke, rest stroke, composers, and much more.
00697376 Book/Online Audio (no tab) $16.99
00142652 Book/Online Audio (with tab) $17.99

A MODERN APPROACH TO CLASSICAL GUITAR
by Charles Duncan
This multi-volume method was developed to allow students to study the art of classical guitar within a new, more contemporary framework. For private, class or self-instruction.
00695114 Book 1 – Book Only $8.99
00695113 Book 1 – Book/Online Audio................$12.99
00699204 Book 1 – Repertoire Book Only............$11.99
00699205 Book 1 – Repertoire Book/Online Audio .$16.99
00695116 Book 2 – Book Only $8.99
00695115 Book 2 – Book/Online Audio................$12.99
00699208 Book 2 – Repertoire $12.99
00365530 Book 3 – Book/Online Audio................$14.99
00695119 Composite Book/CD Pack $32.99

100 GRADED CLASSICAL GUITAR STUDIES
Selected and Graded by Frederick Noad
Frederick Noad has selected 100 studies from the works of three outstanding composers of the classical period: Sor, Giuliani, and Carcassi. All these studies are invaluable for developing both right hand and left hand skills. Students and teachers will find this book invaluable for making technical progress. In addition, they will build a repertoire of some of the most melodious music ever written for the guitar.
14023154...$29.99

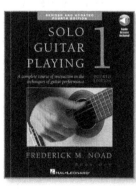

CHRISTOPHER PARKENING GUITAR METHOD
THE ART & TECHNIQUE OF THE CLASSICAL GUITAR
Guitarists will learn basic classical technique by playing over 50 beautiful classical pieces, 26 exercises and 14 duets, and through numerous photos and illustrations. The method covers: rudiments of classical technique, note reading and music theory, selection and care of guitars, strategies for effective practicing, and much more!
00696023 Book 1/Online Audio $22.99
00695228 Book 1 (No Audio) $17.99
00696024 Book 2/Online Audio $22.99
00695229 Book 2 (No Audio) $17.99

SOLO GUITAR PLAYING
by Frederick M. Noad
Solo Guitar Playing can teach even the person with no previous musical training how to progress from simple single-line melodies to mastery of the guitar as a solo instrument. Fully illustrated with diagrams, photographs, and over 200 musical exercises and repertoire selections, these books offer instruction in every phase of classical guitar playing.
14023147 Book 1/Online Audio $34.99
14023153 Book 1 (Book Only) $24.99
14023151 Book 2 (Book Only) $19.99

TWENTY STUDIES FOR THE GUITAR
ANDRÉS SEGOVIA EDITION
by Fernando Sor
Performed by Paul Henry
20 studies for the classical guitar written by Beethoven's contemporary, Fernando Sor, revised, edited and fingered by the great classical guitarist Andres Segovia. These essential repertoire pieces continue to be used by teachers and students to build solid classical technique. Features 50-minute demonstration audio.
00695012 Book/Online Audio $22.99
00006363 Book Only....................................$11.99

HAL•LEONARD®

Order these and more publications
from your favorite music retailer at
halleonard.com

Prices, contents and availability subject to change without notice.

0523
005